D1015308

UNDERSTANDING THE STOCK MARKET

Revised Edition

This book will help you:

- ★ Get started in the stock market
- ★ Understand the daily paper's financial pages
- ★ Protect your current investments and make them grow

THE NO NONSENSE LIBRARY

NO NONSENSE FINANCIAL GUIDES

Understanding the Stock Market, Revised Edition
How to Choose a Discount Stockbroker, Revised Edition
Understanding Treasury Bills, Revised Edition
How to Use Credit & Credit Cards, Revised Edition
Understanding Money Market Funds, Revised Edition
Understanding Common Stocks, Revised Edition
Understanding Mutual Funds, Revised Edition
The New Tax Law & What It Means to You
How to Finance Your Child's College Education, Revised Edition
Understanding IRA's, Revised Edition
Understanding Stock Options & Futures Markets

OTHER NO NONSENSE GUIDES

Car Guides
Career Guides
Cooking Guides
Gardening Guides
Health Guides
Legal Guides
Parenting Guides
Photography Guides
Real Estate Guides
Study Guides
Success Guides
Wine Guides

UNDERSTANDING THE STOCK MARKET
Revised Edition

Arnold Corrigan
& Phyllis C. Kaufman

Longmeadow Press

Understanding the Stock Market, Revised Edition

Cover art © 1984, 1987 by Longmeadow Press.
Design by Adrian Taylor.
Production services by W.S. Konecky Associates, New York.

Published by Longmeadow Press, 201 High Ridge Road, Stamford, Connecticut 06904. No part of this book may be reproduced or used in any form or by any means, electronic or mechanical, including photocopying, recording, or by any information storage and retrieval system, without permission in writing from the publisher.

ISBN: 0-681-40236-9

Printed in the United States of America

0 9 8 7 6 5

To Dugalda Langdon Wolfson, with love

Contents

PREFACE

Your financial security and that of your family depend on making the most of your money now. With as little as $250 or $500 to invest, the NO NONSENSE FINANCIAL GUIDES will introduce you, step by step, into the world of finance.

The NO NONSENSE FINANCIAL GUIDES put you in control.

The NO NONSENSE FINANCIAL GUIDES take the fear out of finance.

Geared toward your financial goals, each easy-to-follow book in the NO NONSENSE series introduces you into a different part of the world of investment opportunity.

Read several NO NONSENSE FINANCIAL GUIDES before you invest. The short time it takes you to read and understand a NO NONSENSE FINANCIAL GUIDE is your first step toward a secure future.

Chapter One

The Stock Market, the World and You

The stock market. To some it's a puzzle. To others, it's a source of profit and endless fascination.

The stock market is the financial nerve center of America. It reflects every change in the economy. It is sensitive to interest rates, inflation, and political events. In a very real sense, it has its fingers on the pulse of the entire world. It is a mirror in which you can see history unfolding day by day.

Taken in its broadest sense, the stock market is also a control center. It is the marketplace where businesses and governments come to raise money so that they can continue and expand their operations. It is the marketplace where giant businesses and institutions come to make and change their financial commitments. The marketplace works with incredible speed and complexity.

The stock market is also a place of individual opportunity. You, as an individual, need ways to protect your savings and make them grow. Because of inflation, you know that each dollar you save today will shrink in real purchasing power over the years. Millions of Americans have found that they could share in the growth of the American economy, and protect themselves against inflation, by investing in common stocks. If you have not yet made that move, you owe it to yourself to learn more about the stock market and stock market investments.

In short, whether you are an investor or not, you owe it to yourself to know more about the stock market and how it works.

This book is planned to help you. As a book about the stock market, it will touch on economics and finance, with some references to history. Perhaps most important, it will help you understand how you can plan a better financial future for yourself.

So, welcome to the world of the stock market and finance.

Chapter Two

The New York Stock Exchange

The phrase "the stock market" means many things.

In the narrowest sense, a stock market is a place where stocks are traded—that is, bought and sold. The phrase "the stock market" is often used to refer to the biggest and most important stock market in the world, the New York Stock Exchange. On the New York Stock Exchange, shares of most leading U.S. corporations are bought and sold. It is one of the greatest financial institutions in history. In 1986, trading volume on the New York Stock Exchange—which we shall refer to from here on as the Exchange or NYSE—reached an average of over $5 billion worth of stocks *per day*.

The NYSE is also a trading place for certain securities other than stocks. For example, it trades bonds, which are debt obligations of corporations. But stocks are the main show.

Both individuals and institutions buy and sell on the Exchange. But you can't walk onto the trading floor ("floor") of the NYSE and buy 100 shares of General Motors for yourself. All buying and selling is done through *brokers* who are members of the Exchange and who function under rules intended to assure that trading will be fair, honest, and free from manipulation.

The Exchange is a not-for-profit corporation run by a board of directors appointed equally from the public and the securities industry. Its member firms are subject to a strict and detailed self-regulatory code. When you give an order to an NYSE member broker to buy or sell shares of a stock for you, you know that your order will be executed according to rules established for your protection.

Self-regulation is a matter of self-interest for stock exchange members. It has built public confidence in the Exchange. It is also required by law. The U.S. Securities and Exchange Commission (SEC) administers the federal securities laws and supervises all securities exchanges. Whenever self-regulation doesn't do the job, the SEC is likely to step in directly.

The Exchange does not buy, sell or own any securities nor does it set stock prices. The Exchange merely is the marketplace where the public, acting through member brokers, can buy and sell at prices set by supply and demand.

2

It costs money to become an Exchange member. There are about 650 memberships or "seats" on the Exchange, owned by large and small firms and in some cases by individuals. These seats can be bought and sold; in 1986 the price of a seat averaged around $600,000. Before you are permitted to buy a seat you must pass a test that strictly scrutinizes your knowledge of the securities industry as well as a check of experience and character. The Exchange guards its reputation carefully.

The volume of trading on the NYSE has climbed from 3 or 4 million shares per day in 1960 to over 140 million shares per day in 1986. This immense growth in volume could never have been accomplished without the innovations of computers and electronic communications. At times there have been predictions that the whole trading process would become automated. But paradoxically, the smooth functioning of the system depends to an exceptional extent on *people* and on the way they function.

How Your Order Is Handled

When you, as an individual, want to place an order to buy or sell shares, you contact a brokerage firm that is a member of the Exchange. A *registered representative* or "RR" will take your order. He or she is a trained professional who has passed an examination on many matters including Exchange rules and procedures.

Your order is relayed to a telephone clerk on the floor of the Exchange and by the telephone clerk to the "floor broker." The floor broker who actually executes your order on the trading floor has an exhausting and high-pressure job. The trading floor is larger than half the size of a football field. It is dotted with multiple locations called "trading posts." Every stock traded on the Exchange is assigned to a specific post. The floor broker proceeds to the post where your particular stock is traded and finds out which other brokers have orders from clients to buy or sell the stock, and at what prices. If the order you placed is a "market order"—which means an order to buy or sell without delay at the best price available—the floor broker sizes up the market, decides whether to bargain for a better price or to accept one of the orders being shown, and executes the trade—all this happens in a matter of seconds.

The Specialist

The Exchange tries to preserve price continuity—which means that if a stock has been trading at, say, 35, the next buyer or seller should be able to execute an order within a fraction of that price (unless some major news has intervened to change the market situation for that stock or for the whole market). But what if a buyer comes in when no other broker wants to sell close to the last price? Or vice versa for a seller? How is price continuity preserved? Enter another individual, the *specialist*.

The specialist is an Exchange member charged with a special function, that of maintaining continuity in the price of specific stocks. The specialist does this by standing ready to buy shares at a price reasonably close to the last recorded sale price when someone wants to sell and there is a lack of buyers, and to sell when there is a lack of sellers and someone wants to buy. For each listed stock, there are one or more specialist firms assigned to perform this stabilizing function. The specialist also acts as a broker, executing public orders for the stock, and keeping a record of "limit" orders to be executed if the price of the stock reaches a specified level (see Chapter 14). Some of the specialist firms are large and are assigned to many different stocks. The Exchange and the SEC are particularly interested in the specialist function, and trading by the specialists is closely monitored to make sure that they are giving precedence to public orders and helping to stabilize the markets, not merely trying to make profits for themselves. Since a specialist may at any time be called on to buy and hold substantial amounts of stock, the specialist firms must be well capitalized.

Block Trading

In today's markets, where multi-million-dollar trades by institutions (i.e., banks, pension funds, mutual funds, etc.) have become common, the specialist can no longer absorb all of the large blocks of stock offered for sale, nor supply the large blocks being sought by institutional buyers. But the securities industry has a history of coming up with creative solutions to trading problems. Over the last several years, there has been a rapid growth in *block trading* by large brokerage firms and other firms in the securities industry. If an institution wants to sell a large block of stock, these firms will conduct an expert and rapid search for possible buyers; if not enough buying interest is found, the block trading firm will fill the gap by buying shares itself, taking the risk of owning the shares and being able to dispose of them subsequently at a profit. If the institution wants to buy rather than sell, the process is reversed. In a sense, these firms are fulfilling the same function as the specialist, but on a much larger scale. They are stepping in to buy and own stock temporarily when offerings exceed demand, and vice versa.

So the specialists and the block traders perform similar stabilizing functions, though the block traders have no official role and have no motive other than to make a profit. It is difficult to see how a computer could take over this risk-taking capacity. A specialist or block trader can go through anxious days after buying a large quantity of a stock if the price goes down. Sometimes a block may be sold at a substantial loss. Knowing when to buy or sell a block, and what price to pay—and making up one's mind in a matter of minutes or even seconds—makes this a high-paid, tension-packed job. And while it's correctly said that the institutions now dominate trading, the extent to which any single institutional order will affect trading and jar prices is, mercifully, kept down by creative arrangements which absorb shocks to the market and emphasize continuity.

The NYSE and the Computer Age

While the Exchange thrives on human functions, it is dependent on today's electronic magic. Computer terminals in every brokerage office have replaced the old "ticker tape" and now report the day's transactions swiftly and efficiently. The push of a button will call up, on the screen, the record of the day's trading in any stock, the latest prices being bid and asked for the stock, and other data. The stock market averages (see Chapter 6) are calculated in a matter of seconds continuously throughout the day and are flashed around the world over these same systems.

The Exchange has also modernized in smaller ways. Years ago, when you bought shares of a stock, you or your broker took possession of one or more *stock certificates*—elegant pieces of paper that proved your ownership of the shares. They were a nuisance to store safely, and had to be surrendered when it was time to *sell* the shares. Every Wall Street back office had its staff of "runners" or messengers who were kept busy delivering stock certificates to be bought or sold. The certificates still move occasionally, but most changes in ownership are now accomplished by computer entries, and the runners now have less to do.

Commission Rates

One reason the Exchange is currently a healthy, flourishing institution is because of a change that was bitterly opposed by many of the members a decade ago. Before 1975, commissions paid to brokers for executing orders were *fixed* according to a uniform schedule set by the Exchange. Every member firm charged the same commission for a given sized trade. While the schedule provided some discount per share on larger-sized trades, the discount wasn't substantial, even though it was obvious to everyone that the cost of executing a large trade was not much more than the cost of executing a small one.

As a result, the institutional customers whose trades were large rebelled and began to execute trades off the NYSE through brokers who were *not* Exchange members and who charged more realistically. (This over-the-counter market for *listed* securities became known as the "third market." See Chapter 3 for more on over-the-counter dealers.) In some cases, the institutions dealt with each other directly, without a broker. A growing percentage of trading in major stocks was being done away from the NYSE.

In 1975, the Exchange, pushed by the SEC, bit the bullet. Over the protests of many members, fixed commission rates were abolished and the era of "negotiated commissions" began. The commissions paid by large customers dropped sharply. In the ensuing years, many small member firms merged or went out of business, as the industry went through a painful restructuring. But after a few years, the volume of trading on the Exchange began to increase strongly and the industry became more competitive than ever.

Do you, as an individual, pay lower commissions than you did before 1975? That depends on what kind of firm you deal with. We'll come back to that subject in Chapter 13.

Chapter Three

The Other Marketplaces

In the previous chapter, we said that the New York Stock Exchange is the marketplace where stocks of most leading U.S. corporations are traded. In fact, the stocks of over 1,500 major companies are listed on the NYSE. But there are other marketplaces for common stocks as well.

The American Stock Exchange ("AMEX"), also located in New York City, is the prime market for close to 800 stocks, mostly of companies smaller than those represented on the NYSE.

There are also "regional" exchanges, of which the best known are the Pacific, Midwest, Boston and Philadelphia exchanges. A sizable portion of the volume traded on these is in "NYSE stocks" that are dually listed on the regional exchanges. In addition, each of these exchanges has its own listings, often of companies in that particular geographical area.

In total volume of common stock trading, the other exchanges are small compared with the NYSE. Trading on the NYSE in 1986 averaged about 140 million shares per trading day, or *over $5 billion* daily. By comparison, daily trading on the AMEX averaged roughly 12 million shares a day (about $175 million), and all the other exchanges combined accounted, on the average, for over 20 million shares daily (about $750 million).

The above figures do not reflect the total importance of certain exchanges. For example, the AMEX and certain of the regional exchanges have become major factors in the trading of stock *options* (see Chapter 5), and for many of the brokers on those exchanges, this trading has become more profitable than executing stock transactions. But common stock trading is, in a very real sense, the principal attraction, and the NYSE continues to predominate.

The Over-the-Counter Market

There is one marketplace in which the volume of common stock trading begins to approach that of the NYSE. In 1986, trading of common stocks "over-the-counter" or "OTC"—that is, *not* on any organized exchange—averaged more than 110 million shares daily. Since many of these stocks are low-priced, the *dollar* volume was not close to that on the NYSE, but the figure is still impressive.

7

What is the over-the-counter market? Actually, the term covers all securities trading that is *not* done on a registered exchange. Most securities other than common stocks are traded over-the-counter. For example, the vast market in U.S. Government securities is an over-the-counter market. So is the money market—the market in which all sorts of short-term debt obligations are traded daily in tremendous quantities. Likewise the "municipal" market —the market for long- and short-term borrowings by state and local governments. And the bulk of trading in corporate bonds also is accomplished over-the-counter.

While most of the common stocks traded over-the-counter are those of smaller companies, many sizable corporations continue to be found on the "OTC" list, including a large number of banks and insurance companies.

As there is no physical trading floor, over-the-counter trading is accomplished through vast telephone and other electronic networks that link traders as closely as if they were seated in the same room. With the help of computers, price quotations from dealers in Seattle, San Diego, Atlanta and Philadelphia can be flashed on a single screen. Dedicated telephone lines link the more active traders. Confirmations are delivered electronically rather than through the mail. Dealers thousands of miles apart who are complete strangers execute trades in the thousands or even millions of dollars based on thirty seconds of phone conversation and the knowledge that each is a securities dealer registered with the National Association of Securities Dealers (NASD), the industry self-regulatory organization which supervises OTC trading. No matter which way market prices move subsequently, each knows that the trade will be honored.

To return to common stocks: There are well over 3,000 different stock issues listed for trading on the NYSE and the other exchanges. But there are as many as 50,000 more publicly owned corporations of various sizes in the U.S. Of these, the stocks of more than 4,000 are traded actively enough to be tabulated by the NASD. For each of these more active issues, one or more dealers act as traders who "make a market" in that stock—that is, stand ready to buy shares of the stock offered by other brokers or dealers, or to sell shares which other brokers or dealers wish to buy.*

---

*A *broker* acts as an *agent* in executing a customer's order and is compensated by a commission. A *dealer* buys and sells a security for his own account (actually owning the security temporarily in the process) and profits from the "spread" between his buying and selling prices. Many firms act in both capacities, and the general technical term for a brokerage firm is "broker-dealer."

Each such trader must continually post the "bid" and "asked" prices at which he or she is willing to buy or sell in moderate quantities, and the NASD supervises to make sure that the spread between bid and asked (which is the source of the market-maker's profit) is not unreasonably wide.

Here too, modern electronics has left its mark. As we shall see in Chapter 7, trading of several hundred leading OTC stocks is now reported in the same detail as trading on the exchanges through the "NASDAQ" automated system maintained by the NASD. Thanks to computer monitors, a trader can now "see" the market for a given OTC stock far more clearly than was possible years ago. By the same token, the details of OTC trading are no longer hidden from the public, and it will be no surprise if public participation in this less-well-known part of the stock market expands rapidly in coming years.

Chapter Four

Categories of Common Stocks

We've said that common stocks are shares of ownership in corporations. There is, of course, much more to be said.

Rights of Stockholders

A corporation is a separate legal entity that is responsible for its own debts and obligations. The individual owners of the corporation—called *stockholders* or *shareholders*—are not liable for the corporation's obligations. This concept, known as *limited liability,* has made possible the growth of giant corporations. It has allowed millions of stockholders to feel secure in their position as corporate owners. All that they have risked is what they paid for their shares—they can't be hauled into court to put up more money if the corporation fails.

As a stockholder (owner) of a corporation, you have certain basic rights in proportion to the number of shares you own. You have the right to vote for the election of directors, who control the company and appoint management. If the company makes profits and the directors decide to pay part of these profits to shareholders as *dividends,* you have a right to receive your proportionate share. And if the corporation is sold or liquidates, you have a right to your proportionate share of the proceeds. (For more information see the NO NONSENSE FINANCIAL GUIDE TO UNDERSTANDING COMMON STOCKS.)

Ways to Classify Stocks

What type of stocks will you find on the stock exchanges? The question can be answered in different ways. One way is by industry groupings. There are companies in every industry, from aerospace to wholesale distributors. (You won't find any breakdown by industry in the newspapers, where the listings are purely alphabetical, but the research sources mentioned in Chapter 10 often give these classifications.) The oil and gas companies, telephone companies, computer companies, auto companies and electric utilities are among the biggest groupings in terms of total earnings and market values. Railroads used to be considered a key grouping, but they have faded in the market as their importance in the economy has diminished.

Perhaps a more useful way to distinguish stocks is according
the qualities and values investors want. If you are going to
come a part owner of a company, what type of company do you
ant to own?

rowth Stocks

he phrase "growth stock" is widely used as a term to describe
hat many investors are looking for. Because the phrase is often
ed loosely, some cynics define a growth stock as "any stock
at goes up." (Once it stops going up, it isn't a growth stock.)
it the phrase has real meaning. People who are willing to take
eater-than-average risks often invest in what we will call "high-
owth" stocks—stocks of companies that are clearly growing
uch faster than average and where the stock commands a
emium price in the market. The rationale is that the company's
rnings will continue to grow rapidly for at least a few more
ars to a level that justifies the premium price.

As an investor, you should keep in mind that only a small
inority of companies really succeed in making earnings grow
pidly and consistently over any long period. The potential
wards are high, but the stocks can drop in price at incredible
tes when earnings don't grow as expected. For example, the
mpanies in the video game industry boomed in the early 1980s,
hen it appeared that the whole country was about to turn into
ie vast video arcade. But when public interest shifted to personal
mputers, the companies found themselves stuck with hundreds
millions of dollars in video game inventories, and the stocks
llapsed.

There is less glamour, but also less risk, in what we will call—
r lack of a better phrase—"moderate-growth" stocks. Typically,
ese might be stocks that do *not* sell at a premium, but where
appears that the company's earnings will grow at a faster-than-
erage rate for its industry. The trick, of course, is in forecasting
hich companies really will show better-than-average growth; but
en if the forecast is wrong, the risk should not be great, assuming
at the price was fair to begin with.

he Tortoise and the Hare

here's a broad category of stocks that has no particular name
it that is attractive to many investors, especially those who prefer
stay on the conservative side. These are stocks of companies in
isinesses that are not glamorous, but that grow in line with the
.S. economy. Some examples are food companies, beverage com-

panies, paper and packaging manufacturers, retail stores, and many companies in assorted consumer fields.

As long as the economy is healthy and growing, these companies are perfectly reasonable investments; and at certain times when everyone is interested in "glamour" stocks, these "non-glamour" issues may be neglected and available at bargain prices. Like the tortoise of the fable, their growth may not be rapid, but it usually is reasonably consistent. Also, since these companies generally do not need to plow all their earnings back into the business, they tend to pay sizable dividends to their stockholders. In addition to the real growth that these companies achieve, their values should adjust upward over time in line with inflation—a general advantage of common stocks that is worth repeating.

Cyclical Stocks

You will hear certain other stocks described as *cyclical.* These are stocks of companies that don't show any clear growth trend, but where the stocks fluctuate in line with the business cycle (prosperity and recession) or some other recognizable pattern. Obviously, you can make money if you buy these near the bottom of a price cycle and sell near the top. But the bottoms and tops can be hard to recognize when they occur; and sometimes, when you think that a stock is near the bottom of a cycle, it may instead be in a process of long-term decline.

Special Situations

There's a type of investment that professionals usually refer to as "special situations." These are cases where some particular corporate development—perhaps a merger, change of control, sale of property, etc.—seems likely to raise the value of a stock. Special situation investments may be less affected by general stock market movements than the average stock investment; but if the expected development doesn't occur, an investor may suffer a loss, sometimes sizable. Here the investor has to judge the odds of the expected development's actually coming to pass.

Part of the excitement of the stock market concerns the different investment approaches that can be selected. Can investment in each of these types of stocks be profitable? Yes. Is it easy? No. Investing takes hard thought and great care. But with study and persistence, the rewards can be great. If you are looking for investment opportunities, and are willing to look hard, the stock market is a good place to examine.

Chapter Five

Other Types of Securities

This book is about the stock market. Thus far we have talked about common stocks, which account for the largest portion of dollar volume traded on the various exchanges.

But you ought to be acquainted with some of the other types of securities that are listed in the financial pages of your newspaper and traded on the stock exchanges or elsewhere. Here are some brief descriptions:

Preferred Stocks

A preferred stock is a stock which bears some resemblances to a bond (see below). A preferred stockholder is entitled to dividends at a specified rate, and these dividends must be paid before any dividends can be paid on the company's common stock. In most cases the preferred dividend is *cumulative*, which means that if it isn't paid in a given year, it is owed by the company to the preferred stockholder. If the corporation is sold or liquidates, the preferred stockholders have a claim on a certain portion of the assets ahead of the common stockholders. But while a bond is scheduled to be redeemed by the corporation on a certain "maturity" date, a preferred stock is ordinarily a permanent part of the corporation's capital structure. In exchange for receiving an assured dividend, the preferred stockholder generally does *not* share in the progress of the company; the preferred stock is only entitled to the fixed dividend and no more (except in a small minority of cases where the preferred is "participating" and receives higher dividends on some basis as the company's earnings grow).

Many preferred stocks are listed for trading on the NYSE and other exchanges, but they are usually not priced very attractively for individual buyers. The reason is that for corporations desiring to invest for fixed income, preferred stocks carry a tax advantage over bonds. As a result, such corporations generally bid the prices of preferred stocks up above the price that would have to be paid for a bond providing the same income. For the individual buyer, a bond may often be a better buy.

Bonds—Corporate

Unlike a stock, a bond is evidence not of ownership, but of a *loan* to a company (or to a government, or to some other organization). It is a debt obligation. When you buy a corporate bond, you have bought a portion of a large loan, and your rights are those of a *lender*. You are entitled to interest payments at a specified rate, and to repayment of the full "face amount" of the bond on a specified date. The fixed interest payments are usually made semiannually. The quality of a corporate bond depends on the financial strength of the issuing corporation; rating agencies such as Moody's and Standard & Poor's publish detailed credit ratings of the companies and the individual issues.

Bonds are usually issued in units of $1,000 or $5,000, but bond prices are quoted on the basis of 100 as "par" value. A bond price of 96 means that a bond of $1,000 face value is actually selling at $960. And so on.

Many corporate bonds are traded on the NYSE, and newspapers carry a separate daily table showing bond trading. The major trading in corporate bonds, however, takes place in large blocks of $100,000 or more traded off the Exchange by brokers and dealers acting for their own account or for institutions.

Bonds—U.S. Government

U.S. Treasury bonds (long-term), notes (intermediate-term) and bills (short-term), as well as obligations of the various U.S. government agencies, are traded away from the exchanges in a vast professional market where the basic unit of trading is often $1 million face value in amount. However, trades are also done in smaller amounts, and you can buy Treasuries in lots of $5,000 or $10,000 through a regular broker. U.S. government bonds are regarded as providing investors with the ultimate in safety.

Bonds—Municipal

Bonds issued by state and local governments and governmental units are generally referred to as "municipals" or "tax-exempts," since the income from these bonds is largely *exempt from federal income tax*. The tax exemption on certain state and local bonds has been curtailed by the Tax Reform Act of 1986, but there is still a broad supply of such bonds that enjoy full federal tax exemption. Tax-exempt bonds are attractive to individuals in higher tax brackets and to certain institutions. There are many different issues and the newspapers generally list only a small number of actively traded municipals. The trading takes

lace in a vast, specialized over-the-counter market. As an offset
o the tax advantage, interest rates on these bonds are generally
ower than on U.S. government or corporate bonds. Quality is
usually high, but there are variations according to the financial
soundness of the various states and communities; here, as with
private corporations, quality ratings are published by Moody's
and Standard & Poor's.

Convertible Securities

A convertible bond (or convertible debenture) is a corporate
bond that can be converted into the company's common stock
under certain terms. Convertible preferred stock carries a similar
"conversion privilege." These securities are intended to combine
the reduced risk of a bond or preferred stock with the advantage
of conversion to common stock if the company is successful.
The market price of a convertible security generally represents a
combination of a pure bond price (or a pure preferred stock
price) plus a premium for the conversion privilege. Many convertible issues are listed on the NYSE and other exchanges, and
many others are traded over-the-counter.

Options

An option is a piece of paper that gives you the right to buy or
sell a given security at a specified price for a specified period of
time. A "call" is an option to buy, a "put" is an option to sell.
In simplest form, these have become an extremely popular way
to speculate on the expectation that the price of a stock will go
up or down. If you are wrong, the option generally becomes
worthless, but at least you know that the most you can lose is
the price you paid for the option. In recent years a new type of
option has become extremely popular: options related to the various stock market averages, which let you speculate on the direction of the whole market rather than on individual stocks. Many
trading techniques used by expert investors are built around options; some of these techniques are intended to reduce risks
rather than for speculation. The leading markets are the Chi-
cago Board Options Exchange (CBOE), the American Exchange,
the Philadelphia Exchange, and the Pacific Exchange.

Rights

When a corporation wants to sell new securities to raise additional capital, it often gives its stockholders *rights* to buy the
new securities (most often additional shares of stock) at an attrac-

tive price. The *right* is in the nature of an option to buy, with a very short life. The holder can use ("exercise") the right or can sell it to someone else. When rights are issued, they are usually traded (for the short period until they expire) on the same exchange as the stock or other security to which they apply.

Warrants
A warrant resembles a right in that it is issued by a company and gives the holder the option of buying the stock (or other security) of the company from the company itself for a specified price. But a warrant has a longer life—often several years, sometimes without limit. As with rights, warrants are negotiable (meaning that they can be sold by the owner to someone else), and several warrants are traded on the major exchanges.

Commodities and Financial Futures
The commodity markets, where foodstuffs and industrial commodities are traded in vast quantities, are outside the scope of this book. But because the commodity markets deal in "futures"—that is, contracts for delivery of a certain good at a specified future date—they have also, by a sort of historical accident, become the center of trading for "financial futures," which, by any logical definition, are not commodities at all.

Financial futures are relatively new, but they have rapidly zoomed in importance and in trading activity. Like options, the futures can be used for protective purposes as well as for speculation. Making the most headlines have been *stock index futures*, which permit investors to speculate on the future direction of the stock market averages. Two other types of financial futures are also of great importance: *interest rate futures*, which are based primarily on the prices of U.S. Treasury bonds, notes, and bills, and which fluctuate according to the level of interest rates; and *foreign currency futures*, which are based on the exchange rates between foreign currencies and the U.S. dollar. Although, as we have said, futures can be used for protective purposes, they are generally a highly speculative area intended for professional and other expert investors.

Chapter Six

Stock Market Averages

After touching on other types of securities, we return to the stock market and to common stocks—the investment that is most likely to be of interest to you. And we will look at the way stock trading is reported in your daily newspaper.

The financial pages of the newspaper are a mystery to many people. But dramatic movements in the stock market often make the front page. In newspaper headlines, TV news summaries, and elsewhere, almost everyone has been exposed to the *stock market averages.*

In a brokerage firm office, it's common to hear the question, "How's the market?" and the answer, "Up five dollars," or "Down a dollar." With 1500 common stocks listed on the NYSE, there has to be some easy way to express the price trend of the day. Market averages are a way of summarizing that information.

Despite all competition, the popularity crown still goes to an average that has some of the qualities of an antique—the Dow Jones Industrial Average, an average of 30 prominent stocks dating back to the 1890s. This average is named for Charles Dow —one of the earliest stock market theorists, and a founder of Dow Jones & Company, a leading financial news service and publisher of the *Wall Street Journal.*

In the days before computers, an average of 30 stocks was perhaps as much as anyone could calculate on a practical basis at intervals throughout the day. Now, the Standard & Poor's 500 Stock Index (500 leading stocks) and the New York Stock Exchange Composite Index (all stocks on the NYSE) provide a much more accurate picture of the total market. The professionals are likely to focus their attention on these "broad" market indexes. But old habits die slowly, and when someone calls out, "How's the market?" and someone else answers, "Up five dollars," or "Up five"—it's still the Dow Jones Industrial Average (the "Dow" for short) that they're talking about.

The importance of daily changes in the averages will be clearer if you view them in percentage terms. When the market is not changing rapidly, the normal daily change is less than 1/2 of 1%. A change of 1/2% is still moderate; 1% is large but not extraordinary; 2% is dramatic. Here are the values of the leading averages on June 30, 1984, and how changes of these magnitudes would have looked in points:

WHAT % CHANGES WOULD HAVE MEANT IN POINTS

	Value 12/31/86	¼%	½%	1%	2%
Dow Jones Industrial Average	1895.95	4.74	9.48	18.96	37.92
Standard & Poor's "500"	242.17	0.61	1.21	2.42	4.84
NYSE Composite Index	138.58	0.35	0.69	1.39	2.77

As you study the financial pages, you'll note that there are also indexes of utility stocks, transportation stocks, and others. They all have their uses; but for your general understanding of the market, they're far less important.

What's important, if you want to know how the market really acted on a given day, is to look at the broad averages. But when someone asks, "How's the market?"—look at the Dow.

Chapter Seven

Reading the Newspaper Quotations

From the market averages, it's a short step to the thousands of detailed listings of stock prices and related data that you'll find in the daily newspaper financial tables. These tables include complete reports on the previous day's trading on the New York Stock Exchange and other leading exchanges. They can also give you a surprising amount of extra information.

Some newspapers provide more extensive tables, some less. Since the *Wall Street Journal* is available nationwide, we'll use it as a source of convenient examples. You'll find a prominent page headed "New York Stock Exchange Composite Transactions." This table covers the day's trading for all stocks listed on the NYSE. "Composite" means that it also includes trades in those same stocks on certain other exchanges (Pacific, Midwest, etc.) where the stocks are "dually listed." Here are some sample entries:

52 Weeks High	Low	Stock	Div	Yld %	P-E Ratio	Sales 100s	High	Low	Close	Net Chg.
52⅞	37⅜	ConsEd	2.68	5.4	12	909	49⅜	48⅞	49¼	+¼
91⅛	66½	GenEl	2.52	2.8	17	11924	u91⅜	89⅝	90	−1
41⅝	26¼	Mobil	2.20	5.4	10	15713	41	40½	40⅞	+⅝

Some of the abbreviated company names in the listings can be a considerable puzzle, but you will get used to them. The three we have picked are no great mystery—Consolidated Edison (an electric and gas utility), General Electric, and Mobil Corp. The excerpt is from the *Wall Street Journal* of Friday, January 9, 1987, and the trading reported is that of Thursday, January 8. This seemed like an interesting day to pick—January 8 was the first day in history when the Dow Jones Industrial Average rose above 2,000.

While some of the columns contain longer-term information about the stocks and the companies, we'll look first at the columns that actually report on the day's trading. Near the center of the table you will see a column headed "Sales 100s." Stock trading generally takes place in units of 100 shares and is tabulated that way; the figures mean, for example, that 90,900 shares of Consolidated Edison, 1,192,400 shares of General Electric, and 1,571,300 shares of Mobil traded on January 8. (Mobil actually was the 12th "most active" stock on the NYSE that day, meaning that it ranked 12th in number of shares traded.)

The next three columns show the highest price for the day, the lowest, and the last or "closing" price. The "Net Chg." (net change) column to the far right shows how the closing price differed from the previous day's close—in this case, January 7.

Prices are traditionally calibrated in eighths of a dollar. In case you aren't familiar with the equivalents, they are:

$$1/8 = \$.125$$
$$1/4 = \$.25$$
$$3/8 = \$.375$$
$$1/2 = \$.50$$
$$5/8 = \$.625$$
$$3/4 = \$.75$$
$$7/8 = \$.875$$

Con Edison traded on January 8 at a high of $49.375 per share and a low of $48.875; it closed at $49.25, which was a gain of $0.25 from the day before. General Electric closed down $1.00 per share at $90.00, but it earned a "u" notation by trading during the day at $91.375, which was a new high price for the stock during the most recent 52 weeks (a new low price would have been denoted by a "d").

The two columns to the far left show the high and low prices recorded in the latest 52 weeks, *not* including the latest day. (Note that the high for General Electric is shown as 91⅛, not 91⅜.) You will note that while neither Con Edison nor Mobil reached a new high on January 8, each was near the top of its "price range" for the latest 52 weeks. (Individual stock price charts, which are published by several financial services, would show the price history of each stock in detail.)

The other three columns in the table give you information of use in making judgments about stocks as investments. Just to the right of the name, the "Div." (dividend) column shows the current annual dividend rate on the stock—or, if there's no clear regular rate, then the actual dividend total for the latest 12 months. The dividend rates shown here are $2.68 annually for Con Edison, $2.52 for GE, and $2.20 for Mobil. (Most companies that pay regular dividends pay them quarterly: it's actually $0.67 quarterly for Con Edison, etc.) The "Yld." (yield) column relates the annual dividend to the latest stock price. In the case of Con Edison, for example, $2.68 (annual dividend) /

$49.25 (stock price) = 5.4%, which represents the *current yield* on the stock.

The Price-Earnings Ratio

Finally, we have the "P-E ratio," or price-earnings ratio, which represents a key figure in judging the value of a stock. The price-earnings ratio—also referred to as the "price-earnings multiple," or sometimes simply as the "multiple"—is the ratio of the price of a stock to the *earnings per share* behind the stock.

This concept is important. In simplest terms (and without taking possible complicating factors into account), "earnings per share" of a company are calculated by taking the company's net profits for the year, and dividing by the number of shares outstanding. The result is, in a very real sense, what each share *earned* in the business for the year—not to be confused with the *dividends* that the company may or may not have paid out. The board of directors of the company may decide to plow the earnings back into the business, or to pay them out to shareholders as dividends, or (more likely) a combination of both; but in any case, it is the *earnings* that are usually considered as the key measure of the company's success and the value of the stock.

The price-earnings ratio tells you a great deal about how investors view a stock. Investors will bid a stock price up to a higher multiple if a company's earnings are expected to grow rapidly in the future. The multiple may look too high in relation to current earnings, but not in relation to expected future earnings. On the other hand, if a company's future looks uninteresting, and earnings are not expected to grow substantially, the market price will decline to a point where the multiple is low.

Multiples also change with the broad cycles of the stock market, as investors become willing to pay more or less for certain values and potentials. Between 1966 and 1972, a period of enthusiasm and speculation, the average multiple was usually 15 or higher. In the late 1970s, when investors were generally cautious and skeptical, the average multiple was below 10. However, note that these figures refer to *average* multiples—whatever the average multiple is at any given time, the multiples on individual stocks will range widely above and below it.

Now we can return to the table on page 19. The P-E ratio for each stock is based on the latest price of the stock and on earnings for the latest reported 12 months. The multiples, as you can see, were 12 for Con Edison, 17 for GE, and 10 for

Mobil. In January 1987, the average multiple for all stocks was very roughly around 15. Con Edison is viewed by investors as a relatively good-quality utility company, but one that by the nature of its business cannot grow much more rapidly than the economy as a whole. GE, on the other hand, is generally given a premium rating as a company that is expected to outpace the economy.

You can't buy a stock on the P-E ratio alone, but the ratio tells you much that is useful. For stocks where no P-E ratio is shown, it often means that the company showed a loss for the latest 12 months, and that no P-E ratio can be calculated. (Of course, you'll also find many stocks that currently pay no dividends.)

Other Stock Tables

Somewhere near the main NYSE table, you'll find a few small tables that also relate to the day's NYSE-Composite trading. There's the table showing the 15 stocks that traded the greatest number of shares for the day (the "most active" list); a table of the stocks that showed the greatest percentage gains or declines (low-priced stocks generally predominate here); and one showing stocks that made new price highs or lows relative to the latest 52 weeks.

You'll find a large table of "American Stock Exchange Composite Transactions," which does for stocks listed on the AMEX just what the NYSE-Composite table does for NYSE-listed stocks. There are smaller tables covering the Pacific Stock Exchange, Boston Exchange, and other regional exchanges.

The tables showing over-the-counter stock trading are generally divided into two or three sections. For the major over-the-counter stocks covered by the NASDAQ quotation and reporting system (see Chapter 3), actual sales for the day are reported and tabulated just as for stocks on the NYSE and AMEX. For less active over-the-counter stocks, the paper lists only "bid" and "asked" prices, as reported by dealers to the NASD.

Shares of *mutual funds* represent a particular type of stock that we haven't yet mentioned. Most newspaper financial sections carry the daily mutual fund price quotations. We'll deal with these in Chapter 15.

Other Tables

Many of the other financial tables are of interest primarily to professionals or experienced investors, or to persons who have

22

specific interest in certain individual securities. But there are me that can tell you a good bit about the state of the world.

It is worth becoming familiar with the daily table of prices U.S. Treasury and agency securities. The Treasury issues are own not only in terms of price, but in terms of the *yield* repre-nted by the current price. This is the simplest way to get a bird's-e view of the current interest rate situation—you can see at a ance the current rates on long-term Treasury bonds, intermediate-rm notes, and short-term bills.

Elsewhere in the paper you will also find a large table showing rices of corporate bonds traded on the NYSE, and a small table selected tax-exempt bonds (traded OTC). But unless you have specific interest in any of these issues, the table of Treasury prices the best way to follow the bond market.

There are other price tables listed. These are generally for ore experienced investors and those interested in taking higher sks. For example, there are tables showing the trading on several ifferent exchanges in listed options—primarily options to buy or ll common stocks (call options and put options). There are tures prices—commodity futures and also interest rate futures, reign currency futures, and stock index futures. There are also *ptions* relating to interest rates and options relating to the stock dex futures.

Chapter Eight

Plan Before You Buy

The preceding chapters have been rather like a travel guide to
Wall Street and the financial markets—describing the different
types of investments that are bought and sold there, and the
markets where they are traded.

It's important to understand these markets because of the role
they play in your own investments and financial planning. But
before we say more about that subject, we want to point out also
that these markets are critical to the functioning of the whole
U.S. economy. Investors can buy stocks, bonds and other securities
freely because they know that these investments can be sold at
any time with equal ease through the huge market mechanism we
have been describing. Without these markets, corporations could
not raise large amounts of money for expansion, and federal and
local governments would be crippled in conducting their operations. When you buy 100 shares of a stock from another investor
who wants to sell, it may seem to be simply a matter of private
convenience. But without the vast financial markets we have been
describing, the U.S. economy could not have the strength and
flexibility that make it so remarkable.

Now, back to your own investments. What must you know
in order to become an investor in securities? In a sense, very
little. You can, if you wish, go to any stockbroker, explain your
financial situation and objectives, and rely on his or her advice.
Or, if you have a large amount to invest, you can ask for investment
advice and management from an investment advisory firm or
bank trust department.

But even if you intend to rely strongly on outside advice, the
more you understand about investments, the better off you will be.
You want to be able to explain your objectives intelligently to a
professional, and you need to understand what the professional
is recommending. As time goes by, you need to be able to judge
whether your investments are going as planned, and whether the
professional is doing the job that he or she is supposed to.

As you move into securities investments, common stocks are
likely to be the most important for you. Eventually, you may
progress to the point of being able to select common stocks for

ourself. That isn't a skill that can be learned overnight. But
e'll spend the next few chapters discussing points that will
elp you have more understanding of common stock investments—
nd that will also help you later if you move on to bonds, options,
nd some of the other possibilities in the securities field.

Chapter Nine

Looking at Common Stocks

When common stock investments are well chosen, they let you
share in the growth and prosperity of leading American corpora
tions and of the whole economy. Also, because you are a part
owner of the corporation's properties and other assets, stocks can
protect you against inflation over the long run as the corporation'
properties grow in value.

But being an owner involves risks, and no one should invest
in common stocks without understanding that there are risks.
First of all, the corporation you invest in may not do well—whic
may mean that your research wasn't adequate, or it may be because even the best companies can sometimes run into problems
that no one could have anticipated. Second, the whole economy
can go through periods of recession or rapid change that affect
even the best companies. And even if the company and the economy are both in fine shape, the price of your stock is subject to
the broad waves of enthusiasm and disappointment that charac-
terize the stock market, and to minor market fluctuations as wel

Since your object is to make your money grow over the long
run, it isn't enough to know that you are buying the stocks of
quality corporations. You also need to be sure that you are buying
the stocks at attractive *prices*—prices which are reasonable relativ
to the values of the companies and to past experience.

Even if you intend to leave these decisions mainly to professionals, some knowledge on your part, as we said above, will
help. And there is an excitement in learning what is involved
in selecting and managing stocks. Just as the broad movements
of the financial markets can help you to understand what is
going on in the world, so the happenings of individual companie
and industries, and the way professional investors view those
happenings, can give you more understanding of current events
than much of what you read in the news pages.

Investment research involves looking at the whole world,
often from a fresh and different viewpoint. Your thinking must b

- *alert* to news and new developments.
- *flexible* enough to change rapidly when conditions change.

- *thoughtful* enough to consider all information seriously without jumping to conclusions.

There is always an element of judgment involved in trying to estimate the real underlying value of a company, seen either independently or in relation to other companies in the same industry or field. But such judgments can be made. As an investor in common stocks, your objective is to buy stocks for less than these real underlying values—or for substantially less than you estimate the company and the stock will be worth in the future, a few years down the road.

The Company Report

What if someone has recommended a particular stock to you? Or if you yourself have noticed some aspect of a company that makes you think it might be a good investment? One of the best sources of information is the company itself, and particularly its annual report. If you don't have easy access to such reports through a library or brokerage office, find the company address in one of the manuals of companies published by Moody's or Standard & Poor's. (Your local library should have some type of reference manual available.) Write to the office of the secretary of the company and ask for the latest annual and quarterly reports to shareholders. Almost all companies will oblige.

The annual reports of most companies are useful documents, full of information. The primary purpose of the report is to tell you about the events and financial results of the latest year, and a careful reading will tell you a good deal about a company's business. If the company is in more than one basic business, it will give you some idea of the relative importance of the different segments, and of the results that each segment has been achieving. The text will discuss the company's earnings, and any special factors that have been affecting earnings. It should also give some indication of how management views the outlook for the coming year.

The "financial statements" give the figures behind the report, and professional analysts are likely to look at these statements before they consider anything else. It takes experience to understand the investment significance of the statements, but you should at least have a general understanding of what they are all about.

The "statement of income," or "statement of income and

27

expense," is just what the name implies. For each of the last three years, it will show (a) the company's sales or revenues—what it took in; (b) the expenses; and (c) the net income remaining after deducting expenses from revenues.

The expenses may be shown in more or less detail, but in any case they will usually be divided broadly into operating expenses (the actual current expenses of running the business), interest charges, and income taxes. One of the operating expenses, *depreciation*, is different from the others. It is not an actual cash expense, but represents the money that the company sets aside each year to provide for replacing plant and equipment as these wear out. In a year when the replacement outlays are not high, the depreciation set-aside gives the company additional cash to work with, at least temporarily.

The size of the company's debt is shown on a different financial statement, the balance sheet, to be mentioned below. But the *interest charges* shown in the statement of income give you some idea of the impact that this debt has on the company's earnings. In some industries, large borrowings and large interest charges are normal; in others, such figures could be a sign of financial weakness.

The amount of *income taxes* paid by the company is also of special interest. Under the Tax Reform Act of 1986, the basic tax rate on larger corporations is reduced from 46% to 34% (effective July 1, 1987), but many special tax breaks for corporations are reduced or eliminated. If the income tax a company pays is not as high as would be expected, it may mean that the company is in some industry where special tax benefits are provided, such as the oil industry. Or it may mean that the company's taxable income is reduced by certain accounting adjustments, such as additional depreciation charges. In this case, a good analyst will make a judgment as to whether the company's earnings as reported present a fair picture, or whether a more realistic picture is obtained by viewing earnings as they would be if income taxes were up to a more normal level.

One more point of interest about the income statement. In this book we have occasionally talked as if a company's earnings belonged completely to the common stockholders. That isn't always true. If the company has one or more issues of *preferred* stock, the income statement will show the dividends paid on the preferred stock below the figure showing the company's net income. The preferred dividends must be subtracted from net income to find the earnings actually available to the common stockholders. (See Chapter 5.)

The income statement portrays the company's operations over a given year or other period. The "balance sheet," on the other hand, is the *statement of financial condition* which gives a financial picture of the company as of a given date, normally the end of the year or other accounting period.

Here also, we don't intend to analyze the statement in detail, but we will mention a few points that you should watch for. The left side of the balance sheet shows the company's "assets"—what it owns. First are the "current assets," which are defined as cash and other items that either will or can be converted into cash within one year. This category includes the company's inventories (if it is in a business where inventories are required), and its "accounts receivable," the amounts owed to the company by its customers. Usually the value of these items is stated with reasonable accuracy; if the inventories are not worth what they cost, or if there is doubt whether the company's customers will pay their debts, then the company's independent public accountants (also referred to as "auditors") should have required an adjustment on the balance sheet.

The other main category of assets is "fixed assets"—the company's property, plants and equipment. You'll notice that the original cost of the company's plants and equipment is reduced by the aggregate amount of the annual depreciation charges that we mentioned in discussing the income statement. So the depreciation charges serve a double purpose: they provide a set-aside for replacing old plant and equipment, and they result in "writing down" the value of plant and equipment on the balance sheet each year to a more realistic value that takes into account wear and tear and aging.

But even with these adjustments, the real value of a company's fixed assets is often far distant from what is shown on the balance sheet. For example, a company may have bought land years ago for $1 million which is still carried on the balance sheet for that figure but which now has a much higher market value. Or the company may be in a declining industry so that the real value of its plant and equipment, in terms of their earning power and resale value, is far less than the balance sheet shows. The real value of a company's fixed assets can't be discovered directly from the balance sheet, but requires actual appraisal and reevaluation.

On the right-hand side of the balance sheet are the company's "liabilities"—its short-term liabilities, and any long-term debt. An analyst learns to look at a company's debt in terms of what is normal for its industry, and these norms can vary greatly.

Finally, the right-hand side of the balance sheet also shows the "stockholders' equity"—the balance sheet value remaining for the stockholders after the company's liabilities are subtracted from its assets. If the company has one or more issues of preferred stock, the value of these is shown as part of stockholders' equity. What remains is the balance sheet value of the common stock.

The balance sheet value of the common stock usually consists of more than one component. First is the "par value" or "stated value" of the common stock—an accounting designation which, taken by itself, doesn't mean much. Then comes "paid-in surplus" or "additional paid-in capital," which represents amounts above par value that were received by the corporation when it issued its shares. Last comes "retained earnings" or "earned surplus"— the amounts that have been plowed back into the business over the years out of earnings (rather than being paid out as dividends).

These items combined make up the balance sheet value or "book value" of the common stock. Divide this total by the number of common shares outstanding, and you arrive at "book value per share," one of the important figures that professionals look at in trying to judge the real value of a stock. The book value per share isn't usually stated on the company's balance sheet, but it may be shown elsewhere in the report, where various figures are shown summarizing the company's results over a five-year or longer period.

Stocks generally sell in the market at prices very different from their book values—partly because of market factors and partly because the balance sheet values, as we have seen, may not reflect the true value of the company's assets. But book value remains one of the important financial statistics for judging the value of a stock, and a market price that is far above or below book value is sometimes a clue to an overpriced or underpriced stock.

We have only touched the surface of what can be found in a company annual report. If you are tempted to explore further, a good next step is to write to the New York Stock Exchange Publications Department, 11 Wall Street, New York, NY 10005, and ask to order their excellent booklet, "Understanding Financial Statements." (While you're writing, ask for a price list of their other publications for individual investors.)

Chapter Ten

Other Sources of Information

If you want to read further on investment subjects, the supply
of available information is overwhelming. With critical decisions
to be made every day regarding the movement of billions of
dollars, investment managers spend vast amounts for the best data
available, and a whole industry has developed to supply information, statistics and opinions on every conceivable type of investment. Also, numerous books are available in your local bookstore
or library.

Don't neglect the information to be found on the newsstands.
Forbes magazine (twice monthly) makes good reading, and
Barron's weekly is another good source of articles. *Money* magazine carries many articles on investments, and you will also find
interesting articles in business magazines that are less oriented
toward investments, such as *Business Week* and *Fortune*.

When it comes to information on individual companies, you
may have to look in different directions. In the last chapter, we
pointed out that much information is available from the companies themselves. If you are dealing with a full-service brokerage
firm (see Chapter 13), your broker should be able to provide you
with a wide variety of research material. This should include
studies of individual companies and industries prepared by the
firm's research department, and also statistical and research
material compiled by the industry's two leading statistical and
news sources, Moody's and Standard & Poor's.

Moody's and Standard & Poor's both publish encyclopedia-
like manuals that include histories and descriptions of thousands
of companies, and reams of statistics. There are daily or weekly
updates to keep the information completely current. If you want
a quick picture of a company, both services publish individual
pages on all major companies providing condensed descriptions
and statistics. These not only offer a surprising amount of data,
but also give you a clue as to what the experts regard as the most
important facts—the two pages (front and back) function like
a short course in the essentials of security analysis. If you don't
have access to these through a broker, try your library. (If that
doesn't work, you might try to get access to a local business school
library.)

There's one source of investment advice we haven't mentioned. What about all those "hot tip" investment suggestions that almost all of us have gotten at times from friends and relatives? Well—your friends and relatives aren't necessarily wrong. It's always possible that you know someone who is knowledgeable about a particular industry or a particular company. But the investment field is filled with professionals who work full-time screening information and following up possible investment opportunities. In this field, it's hard to compete without great care and hard work. Ideas that seem to promise easy rewards may carry hidden risks. In investing, there's little room for miracles.

Chapter Eleven

The Longs and Shorts of Bulls and Bears

This book is devoted to telling you things you should know about the stock market. In this chapter we've put some assorted things you should know that didn't seem to fit anywhere else.

Bulls and Bears

No discussion of the stock market could be complete without some reference to bulls and bears. A "bull" is an investor who expects the market (or a particular stock) to go up; a "bear" is one who expects it to go down. The origin of the phrases isn't completely clear, but they probably derive from the way each animal fights. A bull lowers its head and tosses its enemy up in the air, while a bear rakes downward on its foe with its claws. A "bull market" is one that is going up, and a "bear market" is one that is going down.

Selling Short

If you are a *bear*, and you think that the market (or a particular stock) is going down, how can you speculate on it? Nowadays that can be done through transactions in options or financial futures. But before these markets existed, the classic bear investment technique was *selling short*. "Selling short" or "short selling" means that you borrow a security and sell it to someone, in the hope that the price of the security will go down so that you can then buy the security back more cheaply and deliver it to repay the loan, making a profit. The technique is recommended to experienced investors only. In the securities industry, you are "long" a security when you own it, and "short" when you don't own it but owe it to someone.

Stock Splits

Stock splits are traditionally viewed as good news for stockholders. But they don't basically mean very much, and now people pay less attention to them than they used to.

Assume that a company has 5 million shares of stock outstanding, selling at around $80 per share, and management thinks that the stock might have better trading markets at the more modest price of $40 per share. The company splits the stock 2-for-1. Now there are 10 million shares outstanding. Each old share has been transformed into two new shares, and the stock is trading around 40. Earnings per share have automatically been cut in half, and the price-earnings ratio remains the same.

No one is really any better or worse off. But the split is usually taken as a signal from management that the company is doing well, and the price of the stock may rise a few points above 40 out of market enthusiasm. In addition, the stock split may be accompanied by a dividend increase—instead of cutting the dividend rate exactly in half, the board of directors may set it at a rate which gives stockholders an effective increase.

The reduced interest in stock splits in recent years is probably related to the greater dominance of institutional stockholders in the markets. The institutions know that a split doesn't really change their interest in the company, and they also know that they may pay relatively lower commission rates when buying or selling stocks that are higher-priced.

Chapter Twelve

New Issues

Up to now, we have talked about the function of securities markets as *trading* markets, where one investor who wants to move out of a particular investment can easily sell to another investor who wishes to buy. We have not talked about another function of the securities markets, which is to *raise new capital* for corporations—and for the federal government and state and local governments.

When you buy shares of stock on one of the exchanges, you are not buying a "new issue." In the case of an old established company, the stock may have been issued decades ago, and the company has no direct interest in your trade today, except to register the change in ownership on its books. You have taken over the investment from another investor, and you know that when you are ready to sell, another investor will buy it from you at some price.

New issues are different. You have probably noticed the advertisements in the newspaper financial pages for new issues of stocks or bonds—large advertisements which, because of the very tight restrictions on advertising new issues, state virtually nothing except the name of the security, the quantity being offered, and the names of the firms which are "underwriting" the security or bringing it to market.

Sometimes there is only a single underwriter; more often, especially if the offering is a large one, many firms participate in the underwriting group. The underwriters plan and manage the offering. They negotiate with the offering company to arrive at a price arrangement which will be high enough to satisfy the company but low enough to bring in buyers. In the case of untested companies, the underwriters may work for a prearranged fee. In the case of established companies, the underwriters usually take on a risk function by actually *buying* the securities from the company at a certain price and reoffering them to the public at a slightly higher price; the difference, which is usually between 1% and 7%, is the underwriters' profit. Usually the underwriters have very carefully sounded out the demand for the securities. But if they have miscalculated, and the demand is disappointing—or if the general market takes a turn for the worse while the offering is under way—the underwriters may be left with securities that can't be sold at the scheduled offering price. In this case the underwriting "syndicate" is dissolved and the underwriters sell the securities for whatever they can get, occasionally at a substantial loss.

The new issue process is critical for the economy. It's important that both old and new companies have the ability to raise additional capital to meet expanding business needs. For you, the individual investor, the area may be a dangerous one. If a privately owned company is "going public" for the first time by offering securities in the public market, it usually does so at a time when its earnings have been rising and everything looks particularly rosy. The offering also may come at a time when the general market is optimistic and prices are relatively high. Even experienced investors can have great difficulty in assessing the real value of a new offering under these conditions.

Also, it may be hard for your broker to give you impartial advice. If the brokerage firm is in the underwriting group, or in the "selling group" of dealers that supplements the underwriting group, it has a vested interest in seeing the securities sold. Also, the commissions are likely to be substantially higher than on an ordinary stock. On the other hand, if the stock is a "hot issue" in great demand, it may be sold only through small individual allocations to favored customers (who will benefit if the stock then trades in the open market at a price well above the fixed offering price).

If you are considering buying a new issue, one protective step you can take is to read the prospectus. The prospectus is a legal document describing the company and offering the securities to the public. Unless the offering is a very small one, it can't be made without passing through a registration process with the SEC. The SEC can't vouch for the value of the offering, but it does act to make sure that essential facts about the company and the offering are disclosed in the prospectus.

This requirement of *full disclosure* was part of the securities laws of the 1930s and has been a great boon to investors and to the securities markets. It works because both the underwriters and the offering companies know that if any material information is omitted or misstated in the prospectus, the way is open to lawsuits from investors who have bought the securities.

In a typical new offering, the final prospectus isn't ready until the day the securities are offered. But before that date you can get a "preliminary prospectus" or "red herring"—so named because it carries red lettering warning that the prospectus hasn't yet been cleared by the SEC as meeting disclosure requirements.

The red herring will not contain the offering price or the final underwriting arrangements. But it will give you a description of the company's business, and financial statements showing just what the company's growth and profitability have been over the last several years. It will also tell you something about the management. If the management group is taking the occasion to sell any large percentage of its stock to the public, be particularly wary.

It is a very different case when an established public company is selling additional stock to raise new capital. Here the company and the stock have track records that you can study, and it's not so difficult to make an estimate of what might be a reasonable price for the stock. The offering price has to be close to the current market price, and the underwriters' profit margin will generally be smaller. But you still need to be careful. While the SEC has strict rules against promoting any new offering, the securities industry often manages to create an aura of enthusiasm about a company when an offering is on the way. On the other hand, the knowledge that a large offering is coming may depress the market price of a stock, and there are times when the offering price turns out to have been a bargain.

New *bond* offerings are a different animal altogether. The bond markets are highly professional, and there is nothing glamorous about a new bond offering. Everyone knows that a new A-rated corporate bond will be very similar to all the old A-rated bonds. In fact, to sell the new issue effectively, it is usually priced at a slightly higher "effective yield" than the current market for comparable older bonds—either at a slightly higher interest rate, or a slightly lower dollar price, or both. So for a bond buyer, new issues often offer a slight price advantage.

What is true of corporate bonds applies also to U.S. government and municipal issues. When the Treasury comes to market with a new issue of bonds or notes (a very frequent occurrence), the new issue is priced very close to the market for outstanding (existing) Treasury securities, but the new issue usually carries a slight price concession that makes it a good buy. The same is true of bonds and notes brought to market by state and local governments; if you are a buyer of municipals, these new offerings may provide you with modest price concessions. If the quality is what you want, there's no reason you shouldn't buy them— even if your broker makes a little extra money on the deal.

Chapter Thirteen

You and Your Broker

Knowing which securities to buy, when to buy them and when to sell is as difficult as any other skilled profession. We have tried to point out that it can also be pleasurable and exciting. Eventually, you may want to try to manage your own securities investments. But in the beginning, at least, you will probably want to rely on the advice of a professional.

There are a few different ways of doing this. Since there is no such thing as a free lunch, you obviously will pay for the advice. If the advice is good, it will be worth paying for. But in some cases the payment will be clearer than in others.

Think back to Chapters 2 and 3, where we discussed how securities are traded. To buy stocks, you need to deal through a broker. You can't wander onto the floor of the New York Stock Exchange and buy 50 shares of General Electric yourself. A brokerage firm must execute your order. Strictly speaking, execution of orders is what a broker does.

But over the years, brokers have also taken on the function of giving *advice,* and in a typical broker-customer relationship, you may be paying more for *advice* than you are for *brokerage,* even though the charge for advice may simply be built into the commission rates you pay when you buy or sell securities.

Two Kinds of Brokers
In other cases, the charges may be separated more clearly. A little history may be useful. Until 1975, commission rates charged by all brokers on the major exchanges were fixed according to a uniform schedule, and brokerage firms competed primarily in terms of the quality of advice and service that they offered. In 1975, fixed commission rates were abolished, and firms became free to set their own rates. The rates charged to institutions on large transactions came down quickly. But most of the old "full-service" brokerage firms kept the rates charged to individuals close to the old levels and continued to provide generous amounts of advice and research.

Then, a new group of "discount brokers" evolved. They provide brokerage service (execution of orders) and very little else, and their commission rates are generally less than half of those charged by full-service brokers. They are useful if you simply want to give orders to buy and sell certain stocks (or other securities). Their function is *not* to give you advice. (See the No Nonsense Financial Guide, *How to Choose a Discount Stockbroker*.)

Investment Advisers

Before saying more about full-service brokers, we should point out that there are firms called "investment advisers" whose function is *only* to give investment advice, and who charge directly for the advice—usually in relation to the size of the account being advised or managed. Bank trust departments do a very large business functioning, in effect, as investment advisers. There are also many independent advisory firms—you may have heard the names of some of the larger ones, such as Loomis-Sayles, T. Rowe Price, and Scudder, Stevens & Clark. However, most of these advisers don't find it economical to serve the average person. The minimum account size they accept may be $100,000, or $500,000, or even higher.

Note that if you are using an adviser who is only an adviser, you still need a broker actually to execute transactions. But the advisory firm will usually be glad to take care of the brokerage arrangements if you so desire.

Choosing a Broker

Now back to those full-service brokers. You probably know the names of some of the largest ones—Merrill Lynch, Prudential-Bache, Shearson Lehman Brothers, Sears Dean Witter, and so on. Although the industry trend has been toward the larger firms, there are still many small or medium sized brokers, some of them excellent. Picking one that is right for you, out of all those available, may not be easy.

As an average customer of a full-service firm, you deal with an individual account executive or "registered representative" (so-called because he or she is *registered* with the stock exchanges and the NASD). The "registered rep" or "RR"—whom we will refer to simply as "your broker"—draws on the volume of research and recommendations from the firm's research department.

Sometimes this works well for the client; sometimes it doesn't. The firm's research and recommendations may be good or not so good. The individual broker may be more or less experienced, and may or may not have a talent for telling the good from the bad, and for adapting the firm's ideas to the needs of individual clients.

There's usually no simple way to tell how well a brokerage firm, or an individual broker, has done for clients in the past unless you know someone who has had excellent experience with a particular broker. By all means talk to that broker and see if he or she might be right for you. If you walk into a brokerage firm off the street and have a broker assigned to you, be careful. If you have doubts about the broker, or if your first experiences aren't satisfactory, don't hesitate to talk to the firm manager or branch manager about making a switch. See if the conversation gives you a clue as to whether you need merely a different individual broker, or perhaps a completely different firm.

You must also remember that most individual brokers are in a position that involves a potential conflict of interest. For better or worse, the average broker is paid as a salesperson—whose compensation depends primarily on the amount of brokerage commissions generated from buy or sell orders. The more orders a broker executes, the more money he or she makes. The broker may also be under pressure to recommend certain investment products or packages where both the broker and the firm make higher-than-average commissions (see Chapter 12). Under these pressures, it's not always easy for a broker to give impartial advice.

How do you avoid having the broker's needs come ahead of yours? First, most brokers are honest and want to do a good job for their clients. Second, most brokers recognize that the greatest success comes to those who help their clients invest profitably and who have built up a loyal following. Third, good management should work well for both you and your broker. In a well-managed common stock account, you should expect to see reasonably frequent transactions in response to changes in business conditions, research developments, and market prices. So a broker who is alert and watchful should earn enough commissions in the normal course of events without "reaching" for unnecessary transactions.

You shouldn't brood about the conflict-of-interest problem, but you should keep it in mind. One protection may be to deal with a very successful broker who has no particular need to make extra commissions off *you*. But human nature is hard to predict, and it may not be the most successful broker who proves most reliable in putting *your* interests first.

Brokers as Advisers
Some brokerage firms think of themselves primarily as advisers rather than brokers, and many have registered with the SEC in

both forms so that they have the right to charge separately for investment advice. Your brokerage firm may specifically offer you the choice of an *advisory* account (especially if your account is sizable) in which you pay a fee related to the size of the account, and the commission rates you pay are below those paid by a nonadvisory client. If you feel that the firm gives good advice and management services, this arrangement is worth considering.

The advisory account will probably involve giving *discretion* to the firm to buy and sell for you (at their *discretion*). In this case you need to take care that the firm is not leaning, consciously or unconsciously, toward an approach that generates higher commissions. But there can be advantages in having your investments managed for you on a discretionary basis. If a broker or adviser is really acting in good faith as an *adviser,* rather than as a salesperson, the adviser can do a better job for you by spending more time on research and decision-making, and less time on the phone with clients.

Asking the Right Questions

Whatever kind of arrangement you are entering into with any kind of broker or adviser, don't begin until you have had a full interview and have asked every question you can think of about the firm's experience and procedures, the individual broker's experience, and the ability of both of them together to meet your needs, preferences, and objectives. Don't hesitate to ask hard questions about commission rates (see Chapter 14); and if you don't get clear answers, go elsewhere.

Keep in mind that brokers and advisers are strictly regulated by the SEC—both the firms and the individuals. Ultimately, every broker knows that if a customer is treated unfairly, the customer can complain to the SEC—or to the NASD or the various stock exchanges, all of which are considered self-regulatory organizations. It's unlikely that you will ever have to go through such a complaint process. But it's reassuring to know that there's a policeman available if you need one.

Chapter Fourteen

Accounts, Orders and Commissions

There are a few points we'd like to mention about opening
a brokerage account.

Cash Accounts and Margin Accounts

You can open a *cash* account and buy securities for cash, which
simply means that you pay in full for what you buy. Or, if you
wish to take more risk, you can open a *margin* account and "buy
on margin," which means that you put up only a part of the cost,
and the brokerage firm lends you the rest and charges you interest.
As of 1986, the firm could lend you up to 50% of the cost (a limit
which can be changed at any time by the Federal Reserve).

By borrowing 50% of the cost of a stock, the margin arrangement lets you buy twice as many shares with a given amount
of cash. Obviously, this increases your risk—you can now make
twice as much profit or lose twice as much. Margin buying isn't
wise for a beginning investor. You can't open a margin account
with an NYSE firm without investing at least $2,000 of your own
money.

Since you will pay interest (at current rates) to the brokerage
firm on the money borrowed, you presumably expect enough
profit from your investment to offset the borrowing cost. But if
the market price of your stock drops sharply, your account will
become "undermargined"—the brokerage firm will not have
enough protection for its loan to you—and you will receive a
"margin call" requiring you to put up additional cash or securities.
We repeat that margin buying is not for the inexperienced.

Whether you have a cash account or a margin account,
"settlement date" on any ordinary stock transaction is five business
days after "trade date" (exactly one week later, unless a holiday
intervenes). Whatever money you must pay on the purchase (100%
of the cost if cash, 50% if margin) is due at the brokerage firm
by the settlement date. Conversely, when you sell a stock, the
brokerage firm normally won't make payment to you before settlement date, since that is the date on which the firm "settles" the
trade with the opposing broker and gets paid for the sale.

Placing Your Orders

When you place an order with a broker to buy or sell a stock, you have certain choices. You can buy or sell "at the market," which means at the best price the broker can get for you at that time. Or you can place a "limit" order, under which you buy only if the price dips to a specified level, or sell only if it rises to a specified level. If you place a limit order, it can be for that day only, for a week or a month; or it can be "open" or "good till cancelled" ("GTC"), which means that the order stays on the books until it is executed or until you cancel it.

Less commonly used, but worth knowing about, are "stop" orders, which can be used to protect a profit or limit a loss. A stop order becomes a market order when the price of a stock reaches or sells through a specified point. For example, if you have bought a stock at 40 and the market price rises to 55, you might place a "sell stop" order at 50 to assure yourself a minimum profit of around 10 points. If the market price dips to 50 or below, your "sell stop" order becomes a market order to sell, and would be executed immediately at the best price available—presumably close to 50, though in a rapidly falling market it might be substantially lower. Similarly, if you bought the stock at 40 and it did not do well, you might place a "sell stop" order at 35 to limit your loss to around 5 points.

These orders point up another function of the specialist. Limit orders and stop orders, by their nature, aren't meant to be executed immediately. Your broker, obviously, can't wait around a particular trading post indefinitely watching the price of your stock. So he or she gives that type of order to the specialist in that stock. It is entered into the specialist's "book" and is executed for your broker when and if the price reaches the specified level.

Odd Lots

We stated earlier that stocks normally trade in units of 100 shares. These are called "round lots." There are also arrangements that let you buy "odd lots" of from 1 to 99 shares. In some cases you may pay 1/8-point over the current round-lot market price on a purchase, or receive 1/8-point less on a sale. You shouldn't let the 1/8-point distress you, but you should remember that the *commissions* on all small transactions tend to be relatively high in percentage terms and can perceptibly reduce your profit (or add to your loss) on a trade.

Commission Rates

Commission rates on stocks are usually based on some combination of the number of shares traded, the price per share, and the total dollar amount involved. The formulas vary widely from broker to broker. Many of the full-service brokers still use a scale based on the rates that were in effect prior to 1975, with adjustments in one direction or another.

The following is a rough generalization of how commission rates stood in early 1987. On trades of from $3,000 to $5,000, the average commission charged by a full-service broker might have been between 2% and 3% of the dollar value (say $60 to $90 on a $3,000 trade). At a discount broker, rates in this range averaged roughly 1% to 1¼% (say $30 to $40 on $3,000). On a trade of $20,000, a full-service broker might have charged you 1½% to 2% ($300 to $400), while discount brokerage rates might have averaged about ½% ($100).

Do these differences mean that you shouldn't use a full-service broker? Not at all, if you can profit from the advice and the service. But if your trading over the course of a year is heavy, you should be aware of the commission costs. You should also recognize the relatively high cost of trading in small or even moderate amounts. We saw that full-service commissions might be in the 2%–3% area on trades of $3,000 to $5,000. If you buy this amount of stock and later sell it, the commissions both ways might total 5% of the value of the stock. Even if the trade is profitable, the 5% cost of going in and out is likely to subtract noticeably from the result.

Does this mean that the investor who has only small capital to work with is at a disadvantage? Yes, it does. But in the next chapter we'll discuss a different investing approach that gets around this problem neatly and that should be of interest to small and large investors alike.

Chapter Fifteen

A Different Approach: Mutual Funds

Up until now, we have described the ways in which securities are bought directly, and we have discussed how you can make such investments through a brokerage account.

But a brokerage account is not the only way to invest. For many investors, a brokerage account has disadvantages—the difficulty of selecting an individual broker, the commission costs (especially on small transactions), and the need to be involved in decisions that many would prefer to leave to professionals. For people who feel this way, there is an excellent alternative available—mutual funds.

It isn't easy to manage a small investment account effectively. A mutual fund gets around this problem by pooling the money of many investors so that it can be managed efficiently and economically as a single large unit. The best-known type of mutual fund is probably the money market fund, where the pool is invested for complete safety in the shortest-term income-producing investments. Another large group of mutual funds invest in common stocks, and still others invest in long-term bonds, tax-exempt securities, and more specialized types of investments.

The mutual fund principle has been so successful that the funds now manage over $400 billion of investors' money—not including over $250 billion in the money market funds. (For a full discussion of mutual funds, read the No Nonsense Financial Guide, *Understanding Mutual Funds*.)

Advantages of Mutual Funds

Mutual funds have several advantages. The first is *professional management*. Decisions as to which securities to buy, when to buy and when to sell are made for you by professionals. The size of the pool makes it possible to pay for the highest quality management, and many of the individuals and organizations that manage mutual funds have acquired reputations for being among the finest managers in the profession.

Another of the advantages of a mutual fund is *diversification*. Because of the size of the fund, the managers can easily *diversify* its investments, which means that they can reduce risk by spreading the total dollars in the pool over many different securities.

(In a common stock mutual fund, this means holding different stocks representing many varied companies and industries.)

The size of the pool gives you other advantages. Because the fund buys and sells securities in large amounts, commission costs on portfolio transactions are relatively low. And in some cases the fund can invest in types of securities that are not practical for the small investor.

The funds also give you *convenience*. First, it's easy to put money in and take it out. The funds technically are "open-end" investment companies, so called because they stand ready to sell additional new shares to investors at any time or buy back ("redeem") shares sold previously. You can invest in some mutual funds with as little as $250, and your investment participates fully in any growth in value of the fund and in any dividends paid out. You can arrange to have dividends reinvested automatically.

If the fund is part of a larger fund group, you can usually arrange to switch by telephone within the funds in the group—say from a common stock fund to a money market fund or tax-exempt bond fund, and back again at will. You may have to pay a small charge for the switch. Most funds have toll-free "800" numbers that make it easy to get service and have your questions answered.

Load vs. No-load

There are "load" mutual funds and "no-load" funds. A load fund is bought through a broker or salesperson who helps you with your selection and charges a commission ("load")—typically (but not always) 8.5% of the total amount you invest. This means that only 91.5% of the money you invest is actually applied to buy shares in the pool. You choose a no-load fund yourself without the help of a broker or salesperson, but 100% of your investment dollars go into the pool for your account.

Which are better—load or no-load funds? That really depends on how much time and effort you want to devote to fund selection and supervision of your investment. Some people have neither the time, inclination nor aptitude to devote to the task—for them a load fund may be the answer. The load may be well justified by long-term results if your broker or salesperson helps you invest in a fund that performs outstandingly well.

In recent years, some successful funds that were previously no-load have introduced small sales charges of 2% or 3%. Often, these "low-load" funds are still grouped together with the no-loads; you generally still buy directly from the fund rather than hrough a broker. If you are going to buy a high-quality fund nd hold it a number of years, a 2% or 3% sales charge shouldn't iscourage you.

Common Stock Funds

Apart from the money market funds, common stock funds make up the largest and most important fund group. Some common tock funds take more risk and some take less, and there is a wide ange of funds available to meet the needs of different investors.

When you see funds "classified by objective," the classifications are really according to the risk of the investments selected, hough the word "risk" doesn't appear in the headings. "Aggresive growth" or "maximum capital gain" funds are those that ake the greatest risks in pursuit of maximum growth. "Growth" r "long-term growth" funds may be a shade lower on the risk cale. "Growth-income" funds are generally considered middle-f-the-road. There are also common stock "income" funds, which ry for some growth as well as income, but stay on the conservative ide by investing mainly in established companies that pay izable dividends to their owners. These are also termed "equity ncome" funds, and the best of them have achieved excellent rowth records.

Some common stock funds concentrate their investments in articular industries or sectors of the economy. There are funds hat invest in energy or natural resource stocks; several that invest n gold-mining stocks; others that specialize in technology, health are, and other fields. Formation of this type of specialized or sector" fund has been on the increase.

Other Types of Mutual Funds

There are several types of mutual funds other than the money market funds and common stock funds. There are a large number f bond funds, investing in various assortments of corporate and overnment bonds. There are tax-exempt bond funds, both long-erm and shorter-term, for the high-bracket investor. There are balanced" funds which maintain porfolios including both stocks nd bonds, with the objective of reducing risk. And there are pecialized funds which invest in options, foreign securities, etc.

The Daily Mutual Fund Prices

One advantage of a mutual fund is the ease with which you can ollow a fund's performance and the daily value of your invest-nent. Every day, mutual fund prices are listed in a special table in the financial section of many newspapers, including the *Wall Street Journal*. Stock funds and bond funds are listed together in a single alphabetical table, except that funds which are part of a major fund group are usually listed under the group heading (Dreyfus, Fidelity, Oppenheimer, Vanguard, etc.).

The listings somewhat resemble those for inactive over-the-counter stocks. But instead of "bid" and "asked," the columns are usually headed "NAV" and "Offer Price." "NAV" is the net asset value per share of the fund; it is each share's proportionate interest in the total market value of the fund's portfolio of securities, as calculated each night. It is also, generally, the price per share at which the fund *redeemed* (bought back) shares submitted on that day by shareholders who wished to sell. The "Offer Price" (offering price) column shows the price paid by investors who bought shares from the fund on that day. In the case of a load fund this price is the net asset value plus the commission or "load." In the case of a no-load fund, the symbol "N.L." appears in the offering price column, which means that shares of the fund were sold to investors at net asset value per share, without commission. Finally, there is a column on the far right which shows the change in net asset value compared with the previous day.

Choosing a Mutual Fund
Very few investments of any type have surpassed the long-term growth records of the best-performing common stock funds. It may help to say more about how you can use these funds.

If you intend to buy load funds through a broker or fund salesperson, you may choose to rely completely on this person's recommendations. Even in this case, it may be useful to know something about sources of information on the funds.

If you have decided in favor of no-load funds and intend to make your own selections, some careful study is obviously a necessity. The more you intend to concentrate on growth and accept the risks that go with it, the more important it is that you entrust your money only to high-quality, tested managements.

There are several publications that compile figures on mutual fund performance for periods as long as 10 or even 20 years, with emphasis on common stock funds. One that is found in many libraries is the *Wiesenberger Investment Companies* annual handbook. The Wiesenberger yearbook is the bible of the fund industry, with extensive descriptions of funds, all sorts of other data, and plentiful performance statistics. You may also have access to the *Lipper Mutual Fund Performance Analysis,* an

xhaustive service subscribed to mainly by professionals. It is
ssued weekly, with special quarterly issues showing longer-term
erformance. On the newsstands, *Money* magazine publishes
egular surveys of mutual fund performance; *Barron's* weekly
as quarterly mutual fund issues in mid-February, May, August
nd November; and *Forbes* magazine runs an excellent annual
utual fund survey issue in August. (For additional sources, see
he No Nonsense Financial Guide, *Understanding Mutual
unds.*)

These sources (especially Wiesenberger) will also give you
escriptions of the funds, their investment policies and objectives.
Vhen you have selected several funds that look promising, call
ach fund (most have toll-free "800" numbers) to get its prospectus
nd recent financial reports. The prospectus for a mutual fund
lays the same role as that described in Chapter 12—"New Issues."
t is the legal document describing the fund's history and policies
nd offering the fund's shares for sale. It may be dry reading,
ut the prospectus and financial reports together should give you a
icture of what the fund is trying to do and how well it has
ucceeded over the latest 10 years.

In studying the records of the funds, and in requesting
aterial, don't necessarily restrict yourself to a single "risk" group.
he best investment managers sometimes operate in ways that
ren't easily classified. What counts is the individual fund's record.

Obviously, you will want to narrow your choice to one or
ore funds that have performed well in relation to other funds
1 the same risk group, or to other funds in general. But don't
ush to invest in the fund that happens to have performed best
1 the previous year; concentrate on the record over five or ten
ears. A fund that leads the pack for a single year may have taken
ubstantial risks to do so. But a fund that has made its share-
olders' money grow favorably over a ten-year period, covering
oth up and down periods in the stock market, can be considered
ell tested. It's also worth looking at the year-to-year record to see
ow *consistent* management has been.

You will note that the range of fund performance over most
eriods is quite wide. Don't be surprised. As we have stressed,
anaging investments is a difficult art. Fund managers are
enerally experienced professionals, but their records have never-
eless ranged from remarkably good to mediocre and, in a few
ases, quite poor. Pick carefully.

Chapter Sixteen

Can You Beat the Averages?

We have discussed how you can select a mutual fund for your investments, and we have also discussed selecting a broker. But in terms of final results, what do you actually expect these professionals to do for you? For that matter, if you have decided to manage your own investment portfolio, what do you expect to do for yourself?

In investing, as in any other activity, it's wise to have clear goals in mind and to pause periodically to see if your results meet your goals. If you are investing in common stocks, either directly or through common stock mutual funds, the most obvious measures of performance comparison are the stock market averages. Depending on your objective, they may not always be a fair measure; but they are a good place to begin.

Performance over the long term means nothing unless it is adjusted to the rate of inflation. If you make your money grow by 8% over a long period, but the rate of inflation is 10%, you will end up with less purchasing power than you had to begin with. So in setting your objectives, you have to keep inflation in mind.

As we said at the very beginning, inflation is one of the prime reasons for selecting common stocks as an investment. Consider that if, for the period 1947–1986, you had invested in all the stocks included in the Standard & Poor's 500 Stock Index, with all dividends reinvested, you would have kept more than 6% *ahead* of the rate of inflation. To put it another way, the *real* purchasing power of your investment would have grown, on the average, by more than 6% a year. Since we are talking about common stocks, the results would have varied very greatly from year to year; but that is how you would have come out over the whole period.

At a 6% growth rate, if the historical trend continues, the value of an investment will double every 12 years. At a real 6% growth rate, $1,000 invested today would have a value after 24 years of *$4,000* in real purchasing power. So in comparing investment performance with the stock market averages, the first point to be made is that simply *keeping even* with the averages should give you very satisfactory results over the long run.

Is it reasonable to hope to do even better? A few stock market theoreticians, especially those with academic backgrounds, have argued that no one can "beat" the market. They have pointed out that the *average* performance of all investment institutions, using professional managers, is generally no better than the market averages. But this misses the point. While the *average* performance of professional managers may be mediocre, there are some who have done *consistently* better than average, and some who have done consistently worse. And there are some amateur investors who, without question, have done better than average over a period of years. Investing may not be easily reducible to a science, but it *is* an art, and it is *not* pure speculation.

It isn't easy to "beat" the averages consistently—certainly not by any wide margin. But a small margin can make a difference over the years. Several good mutual fund managers, for example, have achieved long-term performance records averaging 2% a year ahead of the market averages—that is, more than 8% ahead of inflation. The 2% differential may not seem like much, but it compounds over the years. A $1,000 investment growing at an 8% real rate would have a real value of more than $6,000 after 24 years, compared with $4,000 at 6%.

What are your own prospects for doing this well? The records of mutual fund managements are published in detail, and it's not hard to pick funds that have superior past records. That doesn't guarantee that the funds will perform well in the future—it is up to you to watch and review your holdings regularly—but many of the funds have been remarkably consistent.

It's not so easy to be sure of the past record of a brokerage firm or an individual broker. If you are relying on a broker for advice, you need to review the results regularly and carefully. If you have a common stock portfolio that does not keep pace with the S & P "500" over a period of a year or two, it may be time to consider another broker. (Of course, if you have instructed the broker to be conservative in a bull market, or speculative in a bear market, you shouldn't be surprised at falling behind the averages.)

If you are managing your own portfolio, you need to show the same qualities that you would look for in a professional. You need to be alert to changes in investment conditions, and quick and flexible in your own responses. You need to think for yourself, and not be distracted by fads and crowd enthusiasms.

The average investor is probably happier and better off relying on professionals. But in investing, the rewards go to those who think independently and with originality. If you fit that description, learning to manage your own investments can be exciting and gratifying.

Chapter Seventeen

Can You Beat the Giant Institutions?

Even if you have the personal qualities needed for successful investing, can you hope to beat the institutions? Can you, as an individual, hope to invest successfully in markets that have come to be dominated by institutional giants like banks, pension funds and mutual funds?

The answer, very simply, is *yes*. The institutions haven't been that perfect. There's plenty of room for you.

Certainly the markets have become more sophisticated in recent years—in research, as in other matters. It's harder than it used to be to find a "neglected" stock on the New York Stock Exchange. There are now more research analysts working full-time for institutions. With the help of computers, analysts can screen literally thousands of stocks for positive statistical indicators such as rapid earnings growth, high book value relative to price, high profit margins, etc. Unless you delve into the smaller over-the-counter companies, you aren't likely to find a treasure that hasn't also been found by the professionals.

But once you recognize how the markets operate today, you can find ways of dealing with these problems. First, you have the option of getting professional help yourself from a broker or adviser. A good broker or adviser will understand how the institutions are affecting the general market, or the market for an individual stock, and will help you adjust your own actions accordingly. Or you can go a step further and become a mutual fund shareholder, which means that you have become, in a sense, an institutional investor yourself.

If you are managing your own portfolio, you can be aware of the weaknesses of the institutions, and act accordingly. For all their professionalism, the institutions have often shown a tendency to follow each other and to act, all too often, in a group.

In certain situations, you have to give way. If the institutional analysts agree on liking a certain stock, it will sell high, and if they agree on disliking another stock, it will sell low. You may be basically right about a stock and the institutions may be wrong but, temporarily at least, the market will reflect their views and not yours.

With patience, however, you can turn these tendencies to your own advantage. When the institutions tumble over each other to sell a particular stock, and send the price down sharply, it may be a buying opportunity for you. When they push prices up, it may give you an opportunity to sell at a profit. You can't trade against the institutions thoughtlessly or mechanically without running into danger, but at times their excesses will be opportunities for you.

Fortunately, all the computers in the world are not a substitute for human thought. Computers can perform miracles in summarizing past trends and statistics. But at the critical points where a trend is about to shift and a major change is about to occur—either in an individual stock or in the general market—computers may respond to the change only after the fact, and individuals who can think ahead may walk away with the profits.

Chapter Eighteen

Looking Backward and Forward

Many people view the stock market with apprehension and anxiety. They know that investing in the stock market carries certain risks, but they have no clear idea what the risks are or how large they may be.

Historical memories have a lot to do with these fears. Many people are aware of the period of turmoil that upset the stock market in the mid-1970s. Others remember the much more disastrous crash of 1929 and its aftermath.

The worst collapses in the stock market have always come after the most intense periods of speculation and overenthusiasm. In this respect, nothing within memory has rivaled the boom of the 1920s. Speculation in common stocks during that period was unprecedented. There was virtually no government regulation. People could buy stocks on margin by putting up only 10% of the price and borrowing the other 90%—meaning that they could be wiped out by a 10% dip in market prices. But the opportunities for getting rich quickly and easily seemed unlimited. Stocks were bought on the simple belief that prices would go up endlessly. And prices did go up out of all relation to economic realities.

The end came in late 1929. Within a few months, stock prices tumbled, on the average, by almost 50%, and innumerable paper fortunes were wiped out. As the Great Depression took hold of the U.S. economy, stock prices continued downward for almost three years, in a bear market without precedent. At the bottom, in late 1932, the Dow Jones Industrial Average was down *89%* from its 1929 peak. Throughout the 1930s, both the economy and the stock market managed only a feeble recovery.

After World War II, the memories of 1929 were gradually forgotten. As the postwar economic boom gathered momentum, the stock market entered a golden period—a tremendous rise which stretched from 1949 to 1972 and carried the Dow Jones Industrial Average from a low of 160 in 1949 to a high of over 1,000.

Eventually, speculative attitudes began to return. Again, stocks were bought on the expectation that prices would rise indefinitely. Theories were developed to justify dizzying prices for leading "growth" stocks. Speculation in new companies and new stocks was high.

Although the situation was far less extreme than in 1929, the reckoning was painful. Beginning in early 1973, stock prices entered the worst decline of the postwar period. The decline worsened after the Arab oil embargo struck the world in late 1973, curtailing oil supplies and setting off an historic explosion in oil prices which crippled the growth of the world economy. By late 1974, the stock market averages were down *almost 50%* from their peaks. Many individual stocks were down even more sharply.

Stock prices recovered briskly beginning in 1975, and many investors made substantial money in stocks in the late 1970s and early 1980s, despite some sharp fluctuations. By 1985–86, the market rise broadened and strengthened, and there was little doubt that another major "bull market" was under way—with all the rewards and dangers that a bull market brings. Public interest in common stocks and common stock mutual funds accelerated.

Can It Happen Again?

People still worry about 1929. Could the Great Crash be repeated? We don't think it's possible. There was no government regulation of the securities markets in 1929, and no government support for the economy. Many forms of speculation and market manipulation that prevailed in 1927–29 are not possible today. The government has shown its ability to step in and limit recessions; no administration could ever again stand by and permit a downward economic spiral similar to 1929–32. The economy has built-in stabilizers such as Social Security, unemployment insurance, welfare and other arrangements, which did not exist in 1929. Times have truly changed.

Could the decline of 1973–74 be repeated? That's a very different question, and the answer is—yes, it could happen again, though not easily or frequently. You should be wary in any period when there has been a long boom in the stock market; when price-earnings ratios begin to average above 15; when speculation grows, and investors begin to think that they can make large gains every year. The longer such a situation lasts, and the higher prices go, the more likely it is that the stage is being set for another drastic decline.

During the decade 1975–84, stock prices rose by stages without much sign of excesses of this sort. By 1985–86, however, the continued rise in prices, combined with high trading volume and high volatility, was causing some analysts to warn that the market appeared to be building toward another major peak, which might in turn be followed in time by a major decline.

If you see danger signs of this sort developing, what should you do? First, be exceptionally watchful, even if you think that the peak in the market is some distance away. Second, as the risk of decline seems to grow, don't hesitate to take some (or even all) of your money out of the stock market. Don't be greedy for that last bit of profit; and if the market appears to have passed its peak, don't postpone selling in the hope that prices might get back to their peaks just one more time. Even if you hold only the highest quality stocks and/or the highest quality common stock mutual funds, their market value can shrink rapidly in a severe market decline.

Riding the Waves

It takes moderation and common sense to handle the fluctuations of the stock market. The usual up-and-down cycles in stock prices seem to average about four years in length, but you can't be sure how any particular cycle will behave, and it's never easy to know when a turning point is close.

However, you can avoid certain common mistakes. Many inexperienced investors react to stock market cycles in exactly the wrong way. They buy stocks when the market has been rising for a long time, and people have begun to get over-enthusiastic; and they panic and sell near the end of a decline, just when the market is close to turning up.

To invest for yourself successfully, you need to avoid being caught up by market fads and crowd psychology. When prices have gone up sharply, all the news seems to be good, and everyone is enthusiastic—be cautious. When people tell you that the market is "bound to go up"—be extra cautious. Remember that it's never that easy. When prices have dropped sharply and everyone assures you that they are bound to drop further, try to collect your courage enough to do some buying.

Since it's never easy to outguess the market, consider reducing your risk by spacing out your purchases on a regular schedule. If you invest a certain amount every few months over a period of years, you will do some buying when prices are higher and some when prices are lower, and you will end up with a reasonable cost average.

Above all, set yourself reasonable objectives. Trying to keep your investments moderately ahead of inflation over the long run is a realistic, achievable objective. Trying to make a 50% profit every year will almost certainly get you into trouble. If your capital is small and you find it hard to be patient, remember that even a moderate growth rate compounds dramatically over the years if you can achieve it consistently.

We began this chapter by reminding you of times when the stock market was dangerous for investors. But it's even more important to remember the opportunities the stock market has given to individuals. While promoting the growth of America, it has allowed millions of people of average means to share in this growth and to build better financial futures for themselves.

Because of its importance, the stock market should be a part of everyone's education. Those who stumble into it are often disappointed. Those who enter it thoughtfully and with care have often found it both exciting and rewarding. We wish you both excitement and profit.

HAPPY INVESTING!!!!

GLOSSARY

Adviser—See Investment Adviser.

Asked Price (or *Asking Price*)—The price at which a dealer offers to sell a security.

Asset—Any property owned.

Balance Sheet—The financial statement showing a company's assets, liabilities, and "net worth" (the net equity of its owners). See Chapter 9.

Bear—See Chapter 11.

Bid Price—The price at which a dealer offers to buy a security.

Big Board—The New York Stock Exchange.

Block Trading—See Chapter 2.

Blue Chips—A phrase used to describe stocks of leading companies of the highest quality.

Bond—A long-term debt security issued by a government or corporation promising repayment of a given amount by a given date, plus interest.

Book Value—See Chapter 9.

Broker-Dealer—See Brokerage Firm.

Brokerage Firm—A term including several types of firms in the securities business who usually do business with the public.

Bull—See Chapter 11.

Call—An option to buy. See Chapter 5.

Capital—Wealth invested or available for investment.

Capital Gain—The profit from sale of a security or other asset at a price above its cost.

Cash Account—See Chapter 14.

Common Stock—A security representing a share of ownership in a corporation.

Common Stock Fund—A mutual fund investing primarily in common stocks.

Convertible Bond—See Chapter 5.

Corporate Bond—A bond issued by a corporation. See Bond.

Corporation—A legal entity whose owners, called stockholders or shareholders, enjoy limited liability. See Chapter 4.

Dealer—See Brokerage Firm.

Debenture—A type of corporate bond.

Depreciation—The accounting entry by which a company marks down the value of its plant and equipment every year for wear and tear, and theoretically sets aside funds for replacement.

Diversification—The practice of spreading investments over several different securities to reduce risk.

Dividend—A share of earnings paid to a stockholder by a corporation.

Floor Broker—A broker who actually executes trading orders on the floor of an exchange.

Futures—See Chapter 5.

Going Public—See Chapter 12.

Good Till Cancelled—See Chapter 14.

Growth Stock—See Chapter 4.

GTC—See Chapter 14.

Investment Adviser—An individual or organization in the business of giving investment advice. Investment advisers must be registered with the SEC.

Investment Company—A company in which many investors pool their money for investment. Mutual funds are the most popular type.

Limit Order—See Chapter 14.

Load—The sales charge or commission charged on purchase of some mutual funds.

Margin, Margin Account, Margin Call—See Chapter 14.

Market Order—An order to buy or sell immediately at the best price available.

Money Market Fund—A mutual fund which aims at maximum safety, liquidity, and a constant price for its shares.

Most Active List—See Chapter 7.

Municipal Bond—A bond issued by a state or local government. The interest is exempt from federal income tax.

Mutual Fund—An open-end investment company which pools the investments of many investors to provide them with professional management, diversification and other advantages.

NASD—The National Association of Securities Dealers, Inc. A broad industry organization which, among other things, regulates over-the-counter trading.

NASDAQ—The NASD automated quotation system which tabulates and reports on trading of leading over-the-counter stocks.

Net Asset Value—In a mutual fund, the market value of the securities underlying each share of the fund.

New Issue—See Chapter 12.

No-load Fund—A mutual fund which sells its shares at net asset value, without any commission.

NYSE—The New York Stock Exchange.

Odd Lot—A lot of less than 100 shares of stock. See Chapter 14.

Open-end Investment Company—A mutual fund. Technically called "open-end" because the fund stands ready to sell new shares to investors or to buy back shares submitted for redemption.

Open Order—An order to buy or sell a security which remains in effect until executed or specifically cancelled.

Option—See Chapter 5.

Over-the-Counter (OTC)—See Chapter 3.

Par Value—An arbitrary accounting value given to a stock; of no practical importance.

Portfolio—The total list of investment securities owned by an individual or institution.

Preferred Stock—See Chapter 5.

Price-Earnings Ratio (or *Price-Earnings Multiple*)—See Chapter 7.

Principal—The capital or main body of an investment, as distinguished from the income earned on it.

Prospectus—The official document describing a security being offered to the public and offering the security for sale. (Every mutual fund must have an annually updated prospectus.)

Put—An option to sell. See Chapter 5.

Quotation, Quote—A report of the current bid and asked prices on a security.

Redemption—The procedure by which a mutual fund buys back shares from shareholders on demand.

Red Herring—A preliminary prospectus, not yet cleared by the SEC. See Chapter 12.

Registered Representative—A brokerage firm representative who has passed the necessary exam and qualifications to recommend securities and to take orders from the public.

Rights—See Chapter 5.

Round Lot—The normal trading unit of 100 shares of a stock; or a multiple of 100.

R.R.—A registered representative.

Seat—A membership on an exchange.

SEC—The U.S. Securities and Exchange Commission: the federal agency charged with regulating the securities markets and the investment industry.

Security—General term meaning stocks, bonds and other investment instruments.

Settlement Date—The date on which payment is due for a security trade; for stocks, ordinarily five business days after the trade date.

Short Sale, Selling Short—See Chapter 11.

Specialist—See Chapter 2.

Stock—A security representing an ownership interest in a corporation.

Stock Certificate—See Chapter 2.

Stock Split—See Chapter 11.

Tape—The electronic screen or other device on which stock exchange transactions are shown in sequence as they occur (replacing the old-fashioned "stock ticker" which printed transactions on tape.)

Trade—(Verb) To buy or sell a security. (Noun) The purchase or sale of a security.

Trade Date—The date on which a securities trade is executed.

Trading Post—One of several locations on an exchange floor at which the stocks assigned to that particular location are bough and sold.

Underwriter—An investment firm taking the responsibility of offering new securities to the public. See Chapter 12.

Warrant—See Chapter 5.

Yield—The return on an investment. In securities, the dividends or interest received, usually expressed as a percentage of the valu of the investment.

Index

ABOUT THE AUTHORS

ARNOLD CORRIGAN, noted financial expert, is the author of *How Your IRA Can Make You a Millionaire* and is a frequent guest on financial talk shows. A senior officer of a large New York investment advisory firm, he holds Bachelor's and Master's degrees in economics from Harvard and has written for *Barron's* and other financial publications.

PHYLLIS C. KAUFMAN, the originator of the *No Nonsense Guides*, is a Philadelphia attorney and theatrical producer. A graduate of Brandeis University, she was an editor of the law review at Temple University School of Law. She is listed in *Who's Who in American Law, Who's Who of American Women, Who's Who in Finance and Industry* and *Foremost Women of the Twentieth Century*.